TELEVISION MAN

by

Pauline Francis

First published in 2001

by Anglia Young Books
Anglia Young Books is an imprint of
MILL PUBLISHING
PO Box 55
4 Balloo Avenue
Bangor
Co. Down BT19 7PJ

Illustrations by Robin Lawrie

British Library Cataloguing-in-Publication Data

A catalogue record for this book is available
from the British Library

ISBN 1871173 71 X

Printed in Great Britain by Ashford Colour Press,
Gosport, Hampshire

TELEVISION
MAN

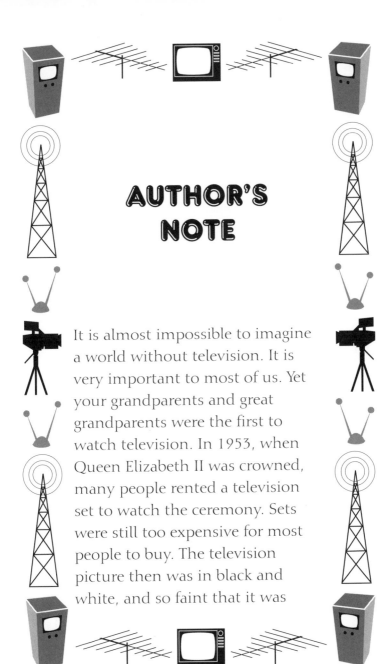

AUTHOR'S NOTE

It is almost impossible to imagine a world without television. It is very important to most of us. Yet your grandparents and great grandparents were the first to watch television. In 1953, when Queen Elizabeth II was crowned, many people rented a television set to watch the ceremony. Sets were still too expensive for most people to buy. The television picture then was in black and white, and so faint that it was

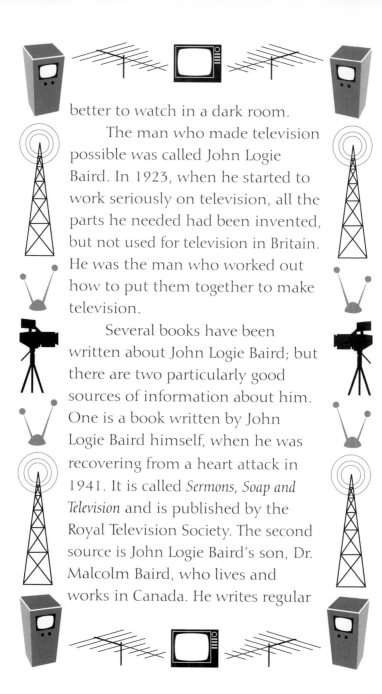

better to watch in a dark room.

The man who made television possible was called John Logie Baird. In 1923, when he started to work seriously on television, all the parts he needed had been invented, but not used for television in Britain. He was the man who worked out how to put them together to make television.

Several books have been written about John Logie Baird; but there are two particularly good sources of information about him. One is a book written by John Logie Baird himself, when he was recovering from a heart attack in 1941. It is called *Sermons, Soap and Television* and is published by the Royal Television Society. The second source is John Logie Baird's son, Dr. Malcolm Baird, who lives and works in Canada. He writes regular

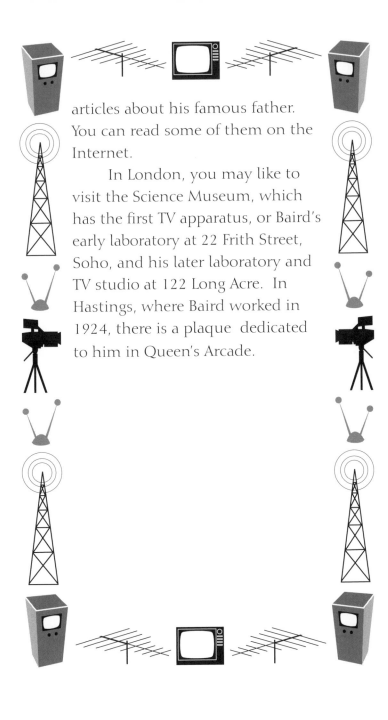

articles about his famous father.
You can read some of them on the
Internet.

In London, you may like to
visit the Science Museum, which
has the first TV apparatus, or Baird's
early laboratory at 22 Frith Street,
Soho, and his later laboratory and
TV studio at 122 Long Acre. In
Hastings, where Baird worked in
1924, there is a plaque dedicated
to him in Queen's Arcade.

CHAPTER ONE:

The Young Inventor

John Logie Baird was born on 13 August,
1888, in Helensburgh, a town about twenty
five miles north west of Glasgow, Scotland.
He was named after his father, the Reverend
John Baird. 'Logie' was the family name
of his great-grandmother, Elizabeth Logie.
Johnnie, as he was called then, had three
older brothers and sisters – James, Annie
and Jean. Johnnie was a healthy little
boy until he was two years old. Then a

serious illness nearly killed him and he was sickly for the rest of his life.

Helensburgh was a pretty town with tree-lined streets and popular with shipowners, architects, engineers and other wealthy people. To the east was the beautiful Loch Lomond, and to the north rose the Scottish Highlands. Unfortunately for John, who was often ill, the winters were wet and bleak.

As a church minister, Mr. Baird did not earn very much money. Life in the family's grey stone house ('The Lodge') was simple and quiet. The house had no electricity, no telephone and no wireless. That was normal for the time. Although all those things had been recently invented or discovered, only very rich people could afford them. The only way of getting about was on foot, on horseback or in horse-drawn buses.

From a very early age, Johnnie often went with his mother to visit sick people in the town. He was shocked by some of the poor families he saw, especially young children who were dressed in sacks tied with string. From that time, he disliked people who wasted their money and who didn't try to help poor people.

Johnnie had a lot of imagination when he was young. He was terrified of ghosts and didn't like going to bed! He was also very easily frightened. One day, Johnnie was peeping out of his bedroom window when he saw an old man in the street below. Johnnie was afraid and ran away from the window. He imagined that he had seen himself as an old man! It was this imagination that helped him later with his inventions.

Johnnie was a happy boy, in spite of his fears and his illnesses. He had plenty of friends and was usually the leader in the games they played. But he was very unhappy at school. His primary school teacher often beat her pupils with a wooden cane. Johnnie's secondary school, Larchfield Academy, made him no happier, although for different reasons. Mr. Baird wanted his son to work in the church, like him. He wanted him to have a Classical education. Instead of learning science, the boys were taught Latin and Greek languages. This would be useful for a life as a church minister. It is hard to believe that science was not taught at all in the school!

This could explain why Johnnie's school reports were not very good. His Christmas report in 1900, when Johnnie was twelve years old, describes him as 'very slow,' 'timid' and ... 'by no means a quick learner.'

However, when Johnnie wasn't at school, he did the things that *really* interested him. From newspapers and magazines, he found out all he could about the new inventions around him – and he carried out many experiments that sometimes got him into trouble.

The telephone had just been invented when Johnnie was born. When he was about thirteen or fourteen, he learned how to make a simple telephone, with string and empty tins, from a magazine called *The Boys' Book of Stories and Pastimes.* But Johnnie wanted a better telephone. He decided to make a telephone system so that he could speak to his friends in their houses. He stretched wires from his house to the houses of four school friends – across roads, over tree branches and round chimney pots! He even made an electric exchange for switching calls from one friend to another. The experiment worked well, but not for long! One of the wires pulled the driver of a horse-drawn bus out of his seat and Johnnie was in great trouble. But within weeks, Johnnie used the same wires to fit electric lights to the family house. It was one of the first houses in Helensburgh to have them, and it was reported in the local newspaper.

At about the same time, Johnnie became very interested in photography. He saved up to buy a camera. Then he built a remote control device which was set off in the middle of the night. In this way, Johnnie had photographs of himself asleep!

The rest of the Baird family became used to strange happenings when Johnnie was around. His sister, Annie, who was rather a serious girl, often wrote about him in her diary. She tells us that Johnnie made her laugh, except when he beat her at chess, because he *always* looked a mess with his blond curly hair sticking up. And he was always dirty from trying to catch his escaping pet rabbits!

Johnnie read all he could about the Wright Brothers who were building flying machines. When he was thirteen, he tried to build an aeroplane with his friend Godfrey Harris. *Their* flying machine looked like two kites joined together and it didn't have an engine. They planned to glide through the air. The two boys climbed out onto a flat roof of the Lodge. Johnnie sat in the glider. He wrote many years later: '...before I had time to give more than one shriek of alarm, Godfrey

gave the machine one terrific push, and I was launched shrieking into the air. I had a very few nauseating seconds while the machine rocked wildly and then broke in half and deposited me with a terrific bump on the lawn.'

Johnnie also read about a simple television experiment in Russia. He wrote many years later: 'It was about this time that the idea of trying to produce television first occurred to me.' Much of his thinking about television was done when he was a schoolboy. He began to carry out very simple experiments himself. In one of them, he tried to make a special cell which uses light to produce electricity (a photo-electric cell). This was to be an important part of his television work some years later. Johnnie managed to produce a small amount of electricity from the cell - and he burned his fingers!

Johnnie was often deep in thought during his teenage years. Whenever his name was mentioned in the family, relatives would smile and say 'puir (poor) Johnnie, puir Johnnie.' A cousin tells us that he was thinking so much at breakfast one morning that he scratched his head with his porridge spoon and made his hair sticky for the rest of the day!

Meanwhile, Mr. Baird dreamed of the day when his son would work for the church as a minister. But Johnnie had other ideas. He wanted to build machines that used electricity. And to do that, he needed to study electrical engineering.

CHAPTER TWO:
Socks, Jam and Soap

Fortunately, Mr. and Mrs. Baird allowed their son do what he really wanted. John Logie Baird went to the Glasgow and West of Scotland College of Technology - now Strathclyde University - a famous college of engineering. At last, John breathed a sigh of relief. Now he could learn about the things that really interested him.

As part of his training, John was sent out to work in engineering workshops.

For the first time, he met working men, men who got their hands dirty at the oily machinery, men who worked all day in noise and heat. John never forgot those times. He started to wear a cloth cap like the working men. He even wore one when he was older and richer.

John Logie Baird was not a very strong young man. He looked sickly and was often ill. At first the workmen teased him because of this and because he was a student. They thought he wouldn't want to get his hands dirty like them. But John always worked hard and the men began to respect him for it.

When John left the College of Technology, in 1911, he went to work at a nearby power station. It was a very tough job. John had to be ready, day or night, to carry out repair work if any of the machines broke down. He started work at five o'clock in the morning and was often ill from walking through the cold, wet streets.

John didn't like his job very much. It was often boring. But as he worked, he thought about new inventions. Like many inventors' ideas, they seemed strange. One day, he decided to try to make diamonds out of the coal dust that lay on the floor of the power station. The experiment needed a lot of electricity. Too much for the power station! John accidentally cut off the electricity supply to most of the city of Glasgow. He left that job soon afterwards!

A much bigger disappointment soon followed. In 1914, the First World War broke out. Men everywhere rushed to join the army. They were proud to fight for their country. John went for an interview. Everything went well until it was time for the medical tests. The doctor wrote on his card: 'Unfit for any service.' John was very upset because he couldn't help his country like his friends.

However, it was his bad health that led John to his first invention, which earned him a little money. He remembered the wet mornings when he had walked through the streets of Glasgow and arrived at work with wet feet. He designed a special sock which kept the feet warm and dry. John hired people to walk about the Glasgow streets wearing a board to advertise his socks. So he also invented the first sandwich board. He made some money, enough to allow him to go to a warmer country.

John's childhood friend, Godfrey, had gone to work on the island of Trinidad, in the West Indies. He wrote to John, 'Come and join me. The sun will be good for you.' John sold his sock company, bought cloth and safety pins to sell, and sailed in 1919. But he couldn't sell his goods in Trinidad. John did not give up. He was always good at making use of what was around him. He began to explore the island and found fruits called guava and mango which he made into jam. Unfortunately, the boiling sugary jam attracted thousands

of insects from miles around! However, John did make enough jam to send back to Britain. His little business did well for about a year and John even kept a locust as a pet. But then he became ill with malaria – a serious illness carried by mosquitoes.

John did not talk about his 'other work' in Trinidad. But seventeen years later, when he was well-known, he admitted in a newspaper article that when he went to Trinidad...'I packed ...a third trunk with books on sound, light, heat, electricity and the latest discoveries that pointed in the direction of my own goal, television.' And he added: 'The only progress I made in that West Indies year was towards television...on my return to England I was ready for new experiments.'

John Logie Baird did more than read in Trinidad. Local people at the time often saw flashing lights inside his house and were frightened. They gave him the nickname of 'Black Magic Man.'

John found that the Caribbean climate wasn't very good for him after all. He sailed back to England and rented a small shop in London. At first he sold his jam. With the money he made from this, he bought a large amount of cheap soap and sold it as 'Baird's Speedy Cleaner.' He merged with a rival business and hoped he would become a successful businessman after all. But John couldn't stand the strain of the business world. He became very ill.

Mr. and Mrs. Baird thought that their son had wasted a good education. They did not realise that he already had in his mind an idea too amazing to talk about. They did not realise that he was trying to earn enough money to pay for a fabulous invention.

All these years, John Logie Baird had been dreaming of one thing: he wanted to use a wireless (radio) to send pictures, as well as sound.

CHAPTER THREE:
The First Television Picture

John didn't know how he was going to earn a living while he worked out his ideas. He didn't have enough energy to run his business properly. And, although he had good ideas, he was not a businessman. John was better left alone to work on the things that he really liked.

But John knew one thing – he *had* to improve his health. The family doctor told him to go away to the sun for a long rest. Once again, an old school friend came to the rescue. Guy Robertson (nicknamed Mephy) invited John to stay with him in Hastings, a town on the south coast of England. John accepted gratefully.

The sun and sea air were good for him. Soon, John was strong enough to take long walks along the cliff tops. He began to think about his future again. What *could* he do? So far he had only made a little money out of socks, jam and soap! John had time, if not the money, to think again about his obsession to send pictures. Could *he* make television work?

He thought, as he had so many times before, about an Italian scientist called Guglielmo Marconi who worked in England. He had invented the 'wireless' or radio. Until then, messages could only be sent through wires. Marconi used invisible radio waves in the air to send sound. He used a transmitter which sent out sound in the form of electrical signals. The signals travelled in the waves to the wireless set.

This read the message and turned it back into sound. In 1906, the first radio broadcast using speech was made. In 1920, Marconi's company broadcast the first British radio programme.

John went through every detail of Marconi's work in his mind. He *had* to find a way of using these waves and electrical signals to send pictures. He knew that the answer lay in the photo-electric cell, like the one *he* had tried to make as a young boy. John knew that he could now buy a good photo-electric cell. And somebody had since invented an amplifier, which increased the amount of electricity from the photo-electric cell.

'Nothing new has to be invented to send pictures,' John muttered to himself, 'it's just a question of finding a way to use what has already been invented.'

John's thoughts came in faster and faster. He knew that he was on the point of an amazing idea. He began to walk more and more quickly. He talked to himself as he walked along and waved his arms in the air as he tried to answer his own questions.

Suddenly, John had the answers. He saw the picture-sending machine in his mind. He left the cliff top and rushed back to his room. Mephy listened in amazement as John said: 'Well, sir, you will be pleased to hear that I have invented a means of seeing by wireless.' His friend replied: 'I hope that doesn't mean you are going to become one of those wireless nitwits. Far better keep to soap.'

John could hardly wait. He had to build his machine NOW! He searched the attic rooms and found nearly all the things he needed – a hat box, a knitting needle, a motor from an old electric fan, some torch batteries, scissors, glue and wire. He went to a scrap yard to buy a cheap photo-electric cell.

John knew that the picture he wanted to send had to be looked at a little at a time (this is called scanning the picture).

In 1884, a man called Paul Nipkow had invented a spinning, or scanning disc. It had holes in it, each in a different position. As the disc spun round, each hole recorded a part, or line, of the picture in front of it. John tore the lid from the hat box and cut holes in it. He quickly made his own Nipkow disc.

He fixed the box lid onto the knitting needle. Then he fixed on the photoelectric cell and the motor. He was ready to begin his experiment. But he still needed a picture to scan. John decided to use just a very simple shape, because his equipment was very simple. He cut out the shape of a white cross and put it in front of the disc. John took a deep breath. His idea *must* work. He switched on the motor. The hat lid began to spin round. The points of light from the picture passed through the holes in the lid to the photo-electric cell. They were changed into electric signals. At the other end of the wire, where the electric signals were received, they were re-arranged in the correct order – this is when the picture of the cross *should* appear.

John could hardly bear to look. And when he did, he saw the faint, flickering picture of the cross.

This was the first television picture.

CHAPTER FOUR:
Bill, Will and William

There was a lot of work to be done now and John had no money. He decided to ask for help. He put this advertisement in a newspaper called the *London Times.* 'SEEING BY WIRELESS: inventor of apparatus wishes to hear from someone who will assist in making working model.'

Many people replied. Soon, John had plenty of helpers. But there was a risk. Other scientists – perhaps some of his helpers – were also working on television projects. They might steal his ideas. John asked each one to work on a small part of the project. They didn't know about each other. In this way, his secret would be safe.

By 1924, John was ready to try to send his picture from his camera to a receiver on the other side of the room, rather than in the same machine. He placed the receiver by his wash basin, three feet away from the camera. To his delight, the picture of the cross appeared clearly.

John decided to go back to London in 1925. There, John faced the biggest test of all. How could he send a picture of a human being? This would be much more difficult. The cross was white, with no shades of dark or light. Our faces are made up of light and dark areas, especially around the eyes and nose. Would his camera be able to cope with this? And even if he did send a picture of a human being, would anyone be able to recognise it?

'I can't expect my friends to sit for hours in front of a camera,' John thought. 'They would complain about the great heat and glare from the lights.' So he found the head of an old ventriloquist's dummy. It was old and battered, but it wouldn't complain. John took away the cross and fixed the head in front of the disc. He called the dummy Bill and he was John's closest friend for some time!

John switched on his machine. Then he stared at Bill's picture on the screen. A shiver ran down his spine. It looked just like a ghost – no eyes and no nose – just a ghostly grinning face. It reminded John of all the ghosts he had imagined when he was a small boy. This time he wasn't frightened, just determined to work harder and make a better picture. The camera couldn't show the difference between the light and dark parts of Bill's face. John needed a better photo-electric cell for that, and it would cost a lot of money.

John hoped that the Marconi Company

would be interested in his work. It was already famous for making wireless sets. But they laughed at his work. Like many other people in the mid-1920s, they thought that television could not be made without an important new invention – and nobody knew what that was yet.

Luckily, a man called Gordon Selfridge heard about his work. He owned the famous store in London. He went to see John. 'I'd like you to come to my store three times a week,' he told John, 'and demonstrate your television. I'll pay you twenty pounds a week.'

John was delighted. He could use the money to carry on his experiments. For the demonstration in the shop, he didn't use Bill, but a tiny doll instead. Perhaps he didn't want to frighten the customers. They were very impressed with the flickering image, although it was only about four inches by two inches (10cm by 5cm).

More and more people heard about John's work. A scientific journal called

Nature even published an article about him. Some people were worried when they read it. Could his machine see through walls? Would it spy on people and take pictures when they weren't looking?

Money was always a problem. A man called Will Day lent John money to carry on with his work. But just when things were going well again, Will refused to lend him any more money. John was desperate. He tried to start a company, Television Limited, but nobody wanted to put money into it.

What could he do? He knew there were people in America doing the same work on television. *He* wanted to be the first. John had to swallow his pride. 'I'll have to ask my father,' he told Mephy. At the age of thirty-seven, he wrote to his father asking for money. However, it was his mother's wealthy relatives who bought shares in his company, giving John five hundred pounds. With the money, he built a better photo-electric cell. Now it was time to take Bill's picture again.

It was 2 October, 1925. John turned on his machine. Within seconds, he jumped up and down with excitement. There on the screen was Bill's face, not pale and ghostly, eyeless and noseless – but a face that looked like a real person.

It was time to scan the face of a human being. John couldn't wait to find a friend. Instead, he ran into the office below his rooms. He rushed in, shouting and smiling and speaking so quickly with his strong Scottish accent that nobody could understand him. John caught hold of the young office boy, William Taynton, pulled him upstairs and sat him in a chair in front of the camera disc. Bright lights dazzled the poor boy.

John turned on the camera, then ran into the room next door where he kept the television receiver and screen. He searched the screen for William's face. It wasn't there! He was a failure after all! John walked slowly back into the other room. He could hardly be bothered to find out what was wrong. He found William crouching in the corner. The boy was so terrified and so hot under the lights that he had run away from the camera!

John gave the boy some money pushed him back in front of the camera again. He ran back to the receiver in the next room and looked at the screen. He saw a clear picture of William's face.

The young office boy was the first living person ever to be seen on television.

CHAPTER FIVE:
Fame at last!

In January, 1926, John told Mephy, 'I'm going to show my work to other scientists. If they see my work, my ideas will be accepted.' John wrote to the Royal Institution. It had been set up in 1799 to spread information about science. It was very important and powerful. Forty members of the Institution accepted John's invitation and climbed the narrow staircase up to his shabby attic rooms.

These important men sat on old wooden chairs. In front of them on the table was a strangest machine they had ever seen – and at the end of it was a dummy's head.

John turned on the machine. Within seconds, the picture of the dummy showed on a screen in front of the audience. Quick as a flash, John turned the disc camera towards his audience, and showed them on the screen. There was no sound, just a picture.

One of the men was so excited that he leaned over the machine and lost some of his long white beard in the spinning disc!

The pictures didn't look much like the television pictures you watch today. They were blurred and they flickered. People's movements were jerky. They were also very small and showed only the head and shoulders. But you could recognise the people and the expressions on their faces. One of the scientists there said:

'Well, Baird has got it right. The rest is only a matter of pounds, shillings and pence.'

Throughout 1926, John carried on demonstrating television to anybody who would come to watch. It was hard work. Not everybody was as polite as those first scientists had been. One man even said, 'He has tricked us. He has hidden a boy behind the television receiver.' Another said: 'Anyone could have done it.'

By February, 1927, John was able to set up a new company with a new business partner, Oliver Hutchinson. People were keen to put money into the business because it was the only company demonstrating television. A journalist, Sydney Moseley, who became a good friend, wrote, 'There will soon be a Televisor receiver in every home, just like the wireless.'

However, the day after the company was formed, bad news came from America. The newspapers reported that the Bell Telephone Company had sent television pictures over two hundred miles, from Washington to New York, even though the company had used one thousand technicians to carry out the transmission. 'I'll have to work faster than ever,' John thought. 'There are rich men in America ready to put a lot of money into television. Britain *must* stay in the lead.'

John never liked the business world. He was happiest when he was working alone on his beloved television. To his horror, the chairman of his new company was an engineer. He started to visit John almost every day, asking silly questions and making impossible suggestions for changing the equipment. John used his imagination to the full to get rid of this man when the company moved offices. John was still very thin at the time, after years of living on very little money – and this chairman was rather large. John made the door of his new laboratory *very* narrow. When the chairman made his first visit, he just managed to squeeze through

the door, but he lost all the buttons from his *waistcoat* and dropped his cigar. He never went back!

John Logie Baird worked harder than ever now. A few months later, he sent television pictures from London to Glasgow, a distance of 435 miles, using only two technicians! Everybody admired his determination, especially the Americans. Then he sent television pictures to New York. These experiments confirmed something that John had always said – that television over a long distance was only a matter of electric power, not any new development of television itself.

By 1929, John Logie Baird was able to

set up another company called Baird International Limited. He earned a good salary and bought a fine house in Box Hill, a beautiful part of Surrey. He knew that it was time to take the next big step. He wanted the public to see his television pictures.

He designed a television set that could be quickly made in a factory. He showed it at a radio exhibition in 1928. An engineer called Plessey saw the set, and worked to improve the design. In the next two years, the Plessey Company built one thousand sets. It was called a Baird Televisor. You could even buy a kit to put your own set together. The picture for the Baird Televisor was made up of only thirty lines. We have 625 lines in our picture today, so you can imagine how blurred these early pictures were. People in Canada saw for themselves a few years ago. They watched a restored 1930 Televisor at a museum exhibition.

The Company set up a small studio at its new laboratories and fixed two tall transmitters onto the roof. Regular television transmissions were sent out to the public. Baird wrote, 'I remember how strange it was to come down from the cold laboratory to the exotic atmosphere of the studio....red nosed comedians applying greasepaint, and colourful figures in wigs and lurid costumes, pianists and violinists rehearsing...all the general chaos of back stage.' It was in this chaos that John met his future wife, Margaret, who was one of the pianists.

At this time, only the British Broadcasting Corporation (the BBC) broadcast wireless programmes to the public. John was keen that it should test out his system of television. Some of the people at the BBC laughed at his flickering pictures. Others made fun of John himself – he was shy and shabby. At first, they refused to take his work seriously. Luckily, a new man was put in charge of the BBC. At last, it agreed to send out the first television broadcast – a quarter of an hour a week,

39

after midnight.

This broadcast was made on 30 September, 1929, from John's London studio. It was very important although there were not many people yet with a television set. There were still only about thirty in the whole of the country. Six were the first Baird Televisors – the rest were sets built by amateurs. Other transmissions followed. Regular broadcasts were made after that for a few hours every evening.

Even today, people appearing on television wear extra make-up so that they appear clearly on the screen. In the first days of television, everybody had to wear very heavy make-up – a blue-black lipstick down each side of the nose, round the eyes, along the eyelashes and the mouth. The rest of the face was whitened! This helped the face to seem clearer on the screen.

Now John began to feel braver about his work. People were starting to think well of him. He suggested something new and bold – a live broadcast from an outdoor sporting event. People were already used to listening to them on the radio. Why not show them what was happening? To his surprise, the BBC agreed.

John decided to film a famous horse race called the Derby. The weather was dry and sunny. John had only one camera and he chose to film the end of the race. He stood near the winning post. Although the broadcast was successful because the picture could be seen, John was disappointed. The picture flickered and the shapes were blurred; but the BBC was pleased.

The following year, John was even more ambitious. Television sets were still too expensive for most people. He decided to show the Derby race at a cinema in London. To make the picture large enough for the big screen, he had to send three pictures and show them side by side. John was shaking with nerves as every seat in the cinema filled up. But he needn't have worried. It was a great success.

It was a very busy year. John also demonstrated the first colour television by placing green, red and blue filters in the television transmitter. He showed pictures of blue flowers and red strawberries in a white basket.

To John's amazement, the BBC gave him permission to broadcast the first television play. It was called *A Man with a Flower in his Mouth* by an Italian writer called Pirandello. There were only two people in the play in head and shoulder close-ups. But it ran for half an hour, and was a very important step in television as entertainment.

At last the BBC could see a future for television. It gave the company a small studio in its own Broadcasting House in London. John Logie Baird was thrilled. He was still ahead in the television race – but only just.

CHAPTER SIX:
Losing the Race

Then, as now, things moved very quickly in the world of science. You always had to remember that there were other clever people carrying out the same experiments - or even better ones. Soon the most serious threat to John came from the development of one of these new inventions - electronic television.

In 1934, two British companies – the Electrical Musical Industries (EMI) and

The Marconi Company joined together in 1934 to develop electronic television. They made electronic parts for the camera and for the television set that received the pictures. As electrons travel very quickly, the electronic scanning camera could scan a picture fifty times a second – much faster than Baird's mechanical scanning. The new cameras were able to produce a picture of 405 lines (very close to ours today). This gave a very clear picture with a smaller and lighter camera.

In spite of this, John was still happy and successful. The Baird Company had now moved to new offices in Crystal Palace, in South London. He invented better methods of scanning to improve his pictures – and he managed to stay popular for a few more years.

The blow came in 1936. The BBC began the world's first public television broadcasts. John Logie Baird saw no reason why his television system shouldn't be chosen. But the BBC was aware of the progress of electronic television. It decided to share the programme time between both systems (alternate weeks), so that the best one could be chosen.

John was bitterly disappointed. He had to carry on waiting. But meanwhile, he was busier than ever. He was given a new studio at Alexandra Palace, in North London. On 2 November, 1936, at three o'clock in the afternoon, the Baird television service opened. John was very nervous, and hot in the smart suit he had been forced to wear.

The day was a great success. After ten years of hard work in shabby rooms, his bad luck had finally come to an end. Television was now becoming a part of everyday life, just as he had hoped. What could go wrong?

One night, a fire broke out in John's laboratory at Crystal Palace. His son, Malcolm, later wrote: 'The Baird family home was about a mile from the Palace and as an infant I was held up at the window to see the blaze, but I have no memory of it.'

Nothing remained of the laboratory. All John's designs, drawings and equipment were burned. Some people thought that the fire had been started deliberately. Now he couldn't maintain the equipment he used in the BBC studio. He was often in trouble when things went wrong with it.

A few months later, John Logie Baird faced an even bigger disappointment. The BBC decided to choose the Marconi-EMI system of television. His television service would be closed down.

But John was a very strong person. He still wanted to fight to keep his company alive. He decided that it would make television sets. The company made a lot of money from them. They were the best sets anywhere – but they used the faster system of Marconi-EMI. The money meant that John could try out other ideas. He decided that if he couldn't reach his public on their Televisors, he would reach

them in the cinemas. Most people didn't yet own Televisors and relied on the wireless and the cinema for their entertainment. John started another company, Cinema Television, which showed live events in many cinemas. It was a great success.

In 1939, war broke out between Great Britain and Germany. This war was to become World War Two and lasted until 1945. Scientists soon realised that the television transmitters were a danger. Their signals, which sent the television pictures, could help German aeroplanes to find their way to bomb Great Britain. The British Government closed the television service down. Of course, nobody bought any television sets. The Baird factory closed down.

'You must go to America,' his friend Sydney Moseley told him, 'it will be safe for your children and you can find money to carry out more research.' John did not go. But he did send his wife and children to Cornwall, away from the

German bombs. He stayed and worked alone in his house near London. When a bomb fell on part of the house, John worked in another room.

He set to work on building a colour television set. He built a two-colour camera. Like most inventors, he always believed that good luck was just around the corner, and his fortune would be made. That thought kept John going. In 1944, he showed his colour television, 'Telechrome', to newspaper reporters. They liked it. But so many terrible things were happening in the war, that it was hardly noticed in the newspapers. And when John died two years later, the house was sold and the equipment disappeared.

During the war years, John's friends at this time were surprised that the British Government did not use his skills for the war effort. But people more recently have read the diaries that John Logie Baird kept during the war years and they show that he often met important military men.

Many people now believe that he might have worked on top secret projects for sending secret signals and for finding ways of detecting submarines. No one really knows the truth about these years. One thing is certain: John Logie Baird *never* gave up his television experiments.

The thought of the end of the war kept John going. At last, in June 1946, the television service started again. John wasn't well, but he managed to set up a big cinema screen to show the soldiers' parades as they returned from the war. It was too much for John. He collapsed and died a few days later. He was only 58 years old.

John Logie Baird was buried in Helensburgh.

* * * * * * * * *

John Logie Baird was a man of great courage and always ready to continue his fight to create television. Although he did not give us television as we know it today, he was the man who made television possible. He also brought television to the attention of the world. This led the bigger and richer companies such as EMI and Marconi to decide to develop television further.

John Logie Baird's vision on the cliff tops was the key point in the development of television. When you next switch on your television set, think of the hat box lid, the knitting needle, the old electric motor, the cheap photo-cell, the dummy called Bill – and a man called John Logie Baird.

IMPORTANT DATES

1875
Bell invents the telephone

1884
Paul Nipkow invents a scanning disc

1888
John Logie Baird is born

1896
Guglielmo Marconi arrives in England
Begins work on a wireless system

1906-11
Baird studies electrical engineering

1919

Baird sails to Trinidad

1922

Baird goes to Hastings, England

1923

Baird begins television experiments

1925

Baird moves to Frith Street,London
Demonstrates his picture in Selfridges

1926

Demonstrates his system to the Royal
Institution

1928

TV picture transmitted to New York

1929

The BBC and the Baird Television
Company begin regular experimental TV
system

1930
The first TV sets (Baird Televisors) are sold

1931
Baird marries Margaret Albu in New York
Televises the Derby horse race

1932
Electronic TV system is shown

1936
Opening of BBC TV service using both
systems

1937
Baird's TV system closes down

1940
'Telechrome' TV is demonstrated

1946
Baird dies